Hardbound Edition
First Printing 1993

ISBN 1-56589-026-4

PRINTED IN HONG KONG

Crystal Clarity
PUBLISHERS
14618 Tyler Foote Road, Nevada City, CA 95959
1 (800) 424-1055

A seed thought is offered for every day of the month. Begin a day at the appropriate date. Repeat the saying several times; first out loud, then softly, then in a whisper, and then only mentally. With each repetition, allow the words to become absorbed ever more deeply into your subconscious. Thus, gradually, you will acquire as complete an understanding as one might gain from a year's course in the subject. At this point, indeed, the truths set forth here will have become your own.

Keep the book open at the pertinent page throughout the day. Refer to it occasionally during moments of leisure. Relate the saying as often as possible to real situations in your life.

Then at night, before you go to bed, repeat the thought several times more. While falling asleep, carry the words into your subconscious, absorbing their positive influence into your whole being. Let it become thereby an integral part of your normal consciousness.

DAY

1

THE SECRET
OF FRIENDSHIP

is exercising discrimination

in your choice of friends;

preferring sincerity over praise,

and loyalty over friendly smiles.

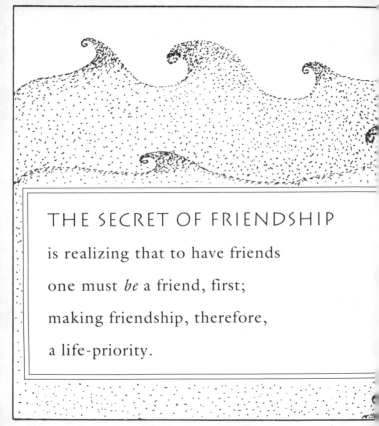

THE SECRET OF FRIENDSHIP

is realizing that to have friends

one must *be* a friend, first;

making friendship, therefore,

a life-priority.

DAY 2

DAY 3

THE SECRET OF FRIENDSHIP

is demanding nothing of others,

but acting and reacting

in a spirit of freedom.

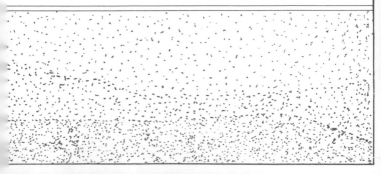

THE SECRET OF FRIENDSHIP

is including other people's happiness

in your own.

DAY

4

DAY 5

THE SECRET
OF FRIENDSHIP

is being more interested

in listening to others than

in getting them to listen to you.

THE SECRET OF FRIENDSHIP

is active, not merely verbal,

concern for the well-being of others.

DAY 7

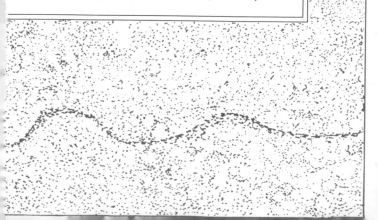

THE SECRET
OF FRIENDSHIP

is liking others, rather than
worrying how well they like you.

THE SECRET
OF FRIENDSHIP

is showing appreciation,

and not taking it for granted

that your friends always know

how you feel about them.

8

DAY

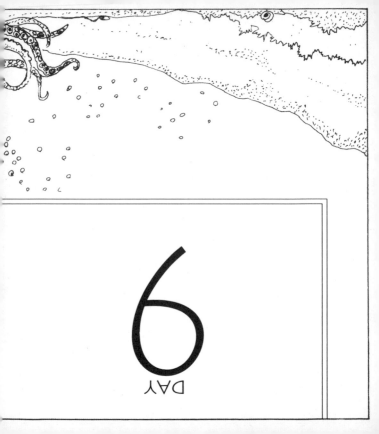

6

DAY

THE SECRET
OF FRIENDSHIP

is accepting your friends as they are,

and not trying to re-create them

in your own image, or according

to your own desires.

THE SECRET
OF FRIENDSHIP

is not imposing your moods,

good or bad, on others,

but giving them the space

to define their own feelings.

DAY

10

DAY 11

THE SECRET
OF FRIENDSHIP

is subordinating your needs

to those of others;

finding in friendship itself

your fulfillment.

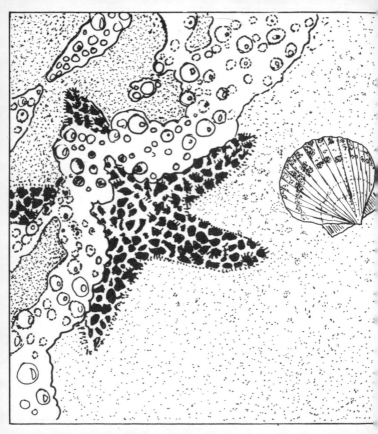

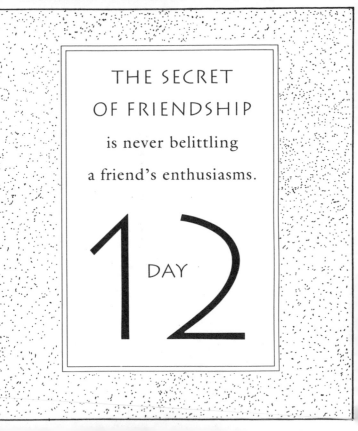

THE SECRET
OF FRIENDSHIP

is never belittling

a friend's enthusiasms.

12 DAY

DAY 13

THE SECRET OF FRIENDSHIP

is courtesy; respecting a friend's right

to his own point of view.

THE SECRET OF FRIENDSHIP

is accepting any differences between you

good-naturedly, and appreciatively.

DAY

14

DAY 15

THE SECRET OF FRIENDSHIP

is expressing kindness with your eyes

and through the tone of your voice,

not only with words.

THE SECRET OF FRIENDSHIP

is sharing with friends

your aspirations and ideals,

and not only passing time with them

in camaraderie.

DAY

16

THE SECRET
OF FRIENDSHIP

is

giving friends your full attention

when conversing with them.

DAY

17

THE SECRET OF FRIENDSHIP

is holding kind thoughts,

especially when misunderstandings occur.

DAY 18

DAY 19

THE SECRET
OF FRIENDSHIP

is never judging, but concentrating

on what attracts you in your friends.

THE SECRET
OF FRIENDSHIP

is not criticizing, but voicing

sincerely the beneficial truth.

DAY 20

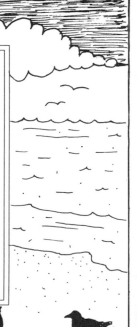

THE SECRET OF FRIENDSHIP

is rejoicing in

a friend's good fortune,

and never drawing

unfavorable comparisons

to your own condition.

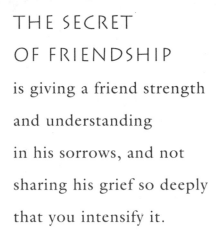

THE SECRET
OF FRIENDSHIP

is giving a friend strength

and understanding

in his sorrows, and not

sharing his grief so deeply

that you intensify it.

DAY

22

DAY
23

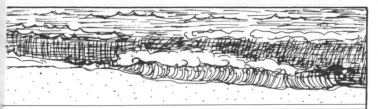

THE SECRET OF FRIENDSHIP

is supporting a friend in the truth,

no less so if it means confessing

your own error.

THE SECRET OF FRIENDSHIP

is reliability; being true to your word,
your promises, your commitments.

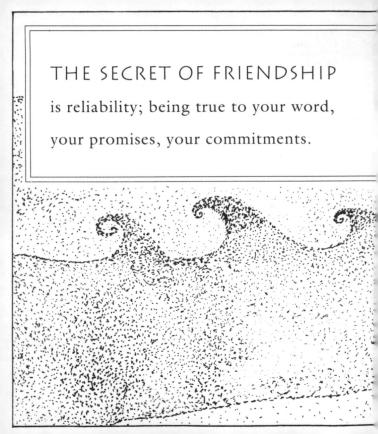

DAY

24

DAY 25

THE SECRET OF FRIENDSHIP

is learning and growing through

your association with others.

THE SECRET
OF FRIENDSHIP

is seeking transcendence

in your relationships.

DAY

26

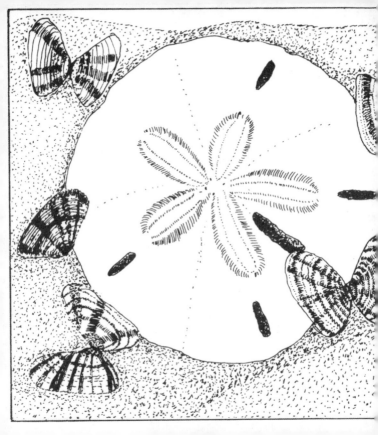

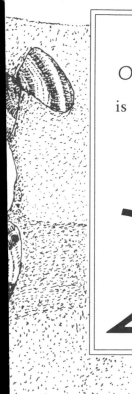

THE SECRET
OF FRIENDSHIP

is loving God above all.

DAY

27

THE SECRET
OF FRIENDSHIP

is seeing God's love

behind the blessing of friendship.

DAY 28

DAY 29

THE SECRET OF FRIENDSHIP

is not emphasizing present tensions in your relationships, but concentrating on the longer rhythms of friendship.

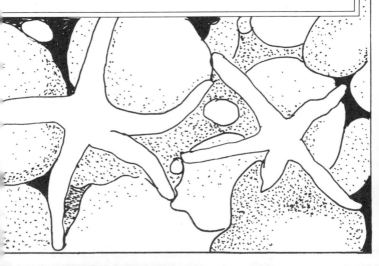

THE SECRET
OF FRIENDSHIP

is loyalty;

being a true friend to others,

even when they let you down.

DAY  30

THE SECRET OF FRIENDSHIP

is seeking benefits

that are mutual,

and never using a friend

for selfish ends.